Soul and Bone

Soul and Bone

Susan Singer Kerschner

Parisburg Publishing

Copyright © 2021 by Susan Kerschner
All Rights Reserved

First Edition

First Printing

Copies available:
www.amazon.com
www.barnesandnoble.com

ISBN: 978-1-61918-061-1

Parisburg Publishing
Pennsylvania USA

Put your ear down close to your soul and listen hard.

— Anne Sexton

To live in this world
you must be able
to do three things:
to love what is mortal;
to hold it
against your bones knowing
your own life depends on it;
and, when the time comes to let it go,
to let it go.

- Mary Oliver, In Blackwater Woods

CONTENTS

IF SILVER WAS METAPHOR
   Heirloom   12
   Unexpected Passage   13

"OPERATION CHOW HOUND" 1945
   The Greatest Generation   16
   Videotape   19
   Bomber Boys   20

THOUSAND EYES OF GOD
   Yom Kippur   24
   Absence of Granite   26
   By Accident   28
   Sycamore Trees   29
   Portrait of a Rocking Chair   30

PERCHED FOR DEPARTURE
   Shards   34
   Soul and Bone   37
   Loss in Four Hues   38
      Green   38
      Red   39
      Midnight Blue   40
      Orange   41
   Perched for Departure   42
   Answering Machine   43
   Early Autumn   44
   Soil to Soul   45
   Seed   46

Swan Song	47
Deciding to Go	48

THINGS I WANTED TO ASK

Only Now	53
When Clothes Don't Make the Man	55
Loss Gathers in Pools of Blue	57
Northbound Canvas	59
Ace of Fire, Six of Water	61
I Am Not This	62
Airborne	63
Careless	64
Torch Thistle	66
1000 Year Flood	67
Dumfoundling Bay	70
C.O.D.	71

MEND WHAT'S BROKEN

Toy Closet	76
Coffee Milkshake	77
Before Reading His Letters	79
The Letters	80

NOTES / PHOTOS	83
ACKNOWLEDGMENTS	91
THE AUTHOR	93

Soul and Bone

IF SILVER WAS METAPHOR

Heirloom

What if silver was metaphor
for impermanence
my father carefully laid out
a lifetime collection
of family silver.

Decide now
whatever you'd like.

I feel him watching me
plod through dinner party history
stories of butlers and cooks
whisper among these piles
of triumphant survivors.

It's no accident
this is what he leaves for us
I lift a shiny gravy boat
inhale the generations
light refracted everywhere
even bent through windows.

Prisms hang like fruit
on the blue tile lamp
withstanding years of use
each bears some small dent.

Making my way around the oval table
I examine every platter and bowl
their properties strong
like my father
begging my caress
my hands long for the soft touch
of one who will leave soon.

Unexpected Passage

I heard the sound of your death
through my sister's phone
we sat frozen on a cement ledge
dog leash in hand
along a small city park
our planned destination null and void.

The moment you ceased to be
triggered expulsion
of my entire torso
a hollowness which caused
me to hold myself imperforate.

Drowning, thrust under
a spigot of words
currents pulled me away from the truth
of what it was like for you to die.

I need to know the facts
of your goodbye
a groan, as your body coaxed you
from the physical earth
waging tug-of-war with your acuity.

Impossible that you could remain
soul here, body there
you moaned in defiance.

Was there a mythic light
while your body was yanked
from this last-stage crypt
what the living invent to mask transition?

I won't know my organs
when they reappear
still perched in that park
impaled on a vortex between life and loss.

"OPERATION CHOW HOUND"
1945

The Greatest Generation

Old men, once bombardiers
tail and ball turret gunners
navigators and pilots full of shrapnel
now fragile bones and ailing prostates
flying human histories in bird formation
twisted upside-down in B-17s
sideways in ocean-dark icy skies,
sometimes go missing in later life.

Young years filled with death nods
flying low missions over Hitler's Third Reich
rust brown roofs of oppressors
and oppressed
maybe over a train scooping up Jews
Theresienstadt happy buildings
hiding false truth optics
to the rest of the world.

Stories of handfuls of rice
divided, shared by five
in a Japanese cell for months
pilots waving brave mid-air goodbyes
between torn off airplane wings.

Generation of aging airmen
who dropped food from the sky
for the starving Dutch
now dropping out of the world
one thousand a day
the living left to battle alone.

2

figure 8s and rectangular course. He told us that <u>all five of us could fly well enough to solo</u>, but that we had to get some stalls, spins and landing in first, of which we haven't done any, hardly. I feel better anyhow, that he said we could do that well. If I can get thru Primary it is a sure cinch I'll get my wings in 4 or 5 months from December since only 1 fellow has washed out Basic from this school. These planes are the reason - they are hot. When they land with their flaps down they look like Stuka Dive Bombers.

← This is what they look like coming in for a landing (much more dihedral, though)

- Steel hale in case of upside down crash
- two open cockpits
- 220 H.P. air cooled Continental Engine
- oleo struts shock absorber — you can't even feel the shock of landing.
- air speed tube (indicator Pitot tube)
- new air corps emblem — also on wings

I am learning a lot about fuselage and cantilever wing construction, at least I have to by tomorrow, so I'll sign off now.

Incidentally, when mom sends me my Gen-lectric razor, include my RED MIT running pants (only the pants). I need them for flying because the leather ones are too hot for low altitude work. Don't forget — just the red pants.

di-dah- di-dit dah-dah-dah-
di-di-di- dah dit
Arnold

P.S.— LOVE ///

Videotape

The remains of my father
captured inside an old videotape
he speaks at podium
recalls piloting body of a plane.

At his first sentence
I am plunged into a place
without protective gear
to fend off anguish

drawing up to his image
my connection is now to machine
like chunks of shell projectile
just as he sat in a frigid
eleven degree B-17G

only now not moving
he looks alive
in this viewing instrument
he tells a funny story

flying close in formation
I poked my wing into my comrade's window
mid-air, fearless

now I rewind
in command of the flight path
knowing the reel will go dark
at the end.

Bomber Boys

Mighty Eighth Air Force crew
put their faith in my father
twenty-one-year-old pilot
as he dives through skies of metal
upside-down Immelmann air loops
to impede Luftwaffe attack.

Within its gray metal machine
diminutive ball turret gunner
crouched in the nose
tail gunner at the back
co-pilot at his elbow
radio operator ready for signal
waist gunner on the planks
engineer-top turret
navigator, bombardier
all present for an 11-hour mission.

Ready aim fire
young men riveted
to one who dips and dives
feathers the engine, toggles switches
one who brought us home every time.

Fifty years later nine men
down to five
passengers on a minibus
ride through museum graveyard
between warplane remnants
navigator targets a safe place to rest his head
relies on his pilot a final time.

Pilot Arnold Singer, Navigator Joseph Hoffman

Immelmann:

Aerobatic maneuvers/flight paths, when the pilot pulls the plane up into the vertical, flips upside-down, then back until he is heading back in the same direction.

THOUSAND EYES OF GOD

Yom Kippur

In the thick of my cancer treatment
I waited for my father to climb the stairs
with 87-year-old legs.

He stretched out beside me
on the queen bed
we listened to the synagogue broadcast
I couldn't go; he didn't want to.

In his abandoned Judaism
decades ago I glimpsed
either fondness or isolated memory
when Koi Nidre began.

I never sat with him in a pew
this bed bearing the weight
my ailing body and his 6'1" length.

He closed his eyes
on the high notes of that holy day
recalled his 13-year-old legs
stepping up to read his Torah portion
child became man
while he inhales bema flowers
reaching the top
eyes open for this moment.

A year later I sit alone
on a wooden synagogue bench
its beige upholstery speckled
with tiny brown dots
resembling the thousand eyes of God.

Forgotten faith recovered
yarmulke, prayer shawl, hymn
lost artifacts of his history
Adonai, Adonai, Adonai
I pretend to hold his bible
inscribed with his young hand
so his name won't die too.

Absence of Granite

I am mourning the absence
of granite
belonging to no one

I hate that my father
is no longer anywhere

his cremated ashes reside
somewhere in the bitter wintry
Santa Fe nights where we left him
it's now 9°F
in the place he loved
for its unforgiving heat
but I am not lured back
to look for his dust
a sign, a trace
an anchor

I wonder where the air has settled him
if his fragments might be blown
into the eye of a tree
tucked in a squirrel's puffy cheeks
or in peeling, ornate grooves
under a bench

maybe his molecules
mingled with mosses
backbone to a leaning branch

I was never one to pay mind to science
but he who has no mass
takes up space within me
as invisible grains
invading my heart.

By Accident

We found your hat
at the top of the closet
left ten years ago

try this one, she said.
like Goldilocks, it fit no one
until now

clothing has a kind of magic
when transferred

your cells commingle with mine
as living testimony

that you have not yet
ceased to exist.

Sycamore Trees

(Platanus occidentals)

As if overnight
trees were stripped
the lawn was scattered with bark shavings

leisurely drive through neighborhoods
meant his announcement in ancient
Latin or Greek
every bush, tree, flower
there was no boundary
to my father's botanical intimacy

aging tree skin pulled away
is just something that happens
yet in its stillness
peelings lying in the yard
are scroll markers
brittle, folded
in embryonic retreat

with his absence comes
a realization of lessons ended
bark now nameless
buried between blades of grass

as if there was a way
to piece together the whole
undo what was taken away.

Portrait of a Rocking Chair

Picture on the mantle
rocking chair on a sea of glass
or a porch
with unmoving palm fronds
intimates old age
or things once in motion
now still

the chair is empty
suggesting departure

artist painted its mirror image
beneath, black shadows invading
the loneliness of one
who may have rested there

every artifact contains an absence
glass half full
empty place at table

in its abstract form
imprint of loss
continues to recede.

PERCHED FOR DEPARTURE

Shards

One heart stops
the other goes to pieces
slivers of moon fallen away
from what shouldn't be detached.

I startle my uncle
boxed reduction of my father
cremated parts of his protector
cradled in thin steel.

Silent sobs shake his head
bowed over words: contained herein
can I hold him? he whispers
from the recent wheelchair.

His grief like a visible spider web
spun on a grouping of fern
moist rain leaves a cloak
eyes darken to deeper brown.

"Taps" trumpets through
southwestern air for our war hero
bagpipes howl in windless skies
as Sandia Mountain pinks
bleed over rocks

tinted like watermelon
in Tiwa Pueblo: *where water slides down*
and shards of the past
seep into desert land in droplets.

The dust of my father
watched mysteriously long
by one eye of a motionless rabbit
witness to tree roots
opening their tendrils to receive.

Howard & Arnold

1944 and 2014

89 years of brother love

Soul and Bone

The noisiness of breath and heart
when crickets cease their night chatter

as if one you loved had never lived
as if shadows were never cast by sunlight

or if no words could be spoken
my tired heartbroken uncle cries out

for his older sibling, remembering
forgetting, then remembering again

seasons pass
sticky shroud of summer dissipates

before fall takes over with stealth
gallops headlong into ice

quiet pierces itself
mountain misses an echo

I wish I could tell my father
your little brother died today

the one who held your soul and bone
as a box of sand.

Loss in Four Hues

Green

My father loved his lush lawn
each wide southern blade of grass
swooned beneath his step
then bending slowly back
skyward determined.

Red

In the sunny breakfast room
we gathered for the lesson
how to section grapefruit
with your special curved knife
no, look; this way, this way
the berries
had to be hulled just right
each one slowly brought to mouth
submerged in powdered sugar
they sat for hours since
he didn't believe food rotted
like milk left out in a pitcher
every drop to be saved
every moment sweetened to taste
ripe with an expiration date.

Midnight Blue

Plane leaving Texas
home where your ashes
were not scattered
flies so low
giant steel belly
seems to graze dotted lights
10,000 feet below
the ordinary seems surreal
up here things appear
in secret pockets
of night turned inside out
somewhere below
woman sits vigil
over ailing parent
someone else readies
to leave his wife for good
young man is taking the dog
for one last walk
beneath thin veneer of cirrus.

Orange

It lies between anger of red
and jaundice yellow of moon

I want to trade something important
to bring you back
so you can view the striking ball of flame
as it kisses earth one last time.

Perched for Departure

Geese don't land
gracefully on a pond

they flap wildly
with reverberating splash

time intervenes
hundreds of suns set

body more broken
day by day

aging is tasteless, odorless
moves forward like a river

birds don't stay long
nothing to keep them here

formulary for your life
get behind the weight of the present

push it forward
when it's time to move on

watch their sleek feathered bodies
prepare for upcoming flight

how do they know
when it's time to go?

Answering Machine

I step into the study
press the Play button
procession of babble begins
missed calls, solicitations, neediness

by some technical glitch
my father's voice
comes across the sound barrier
like horses breaking the finish line

startling me as he tells me
he misses me already
within an hour of leaving
conjuring messages of loss

my heart folds and unfolds
is this mercy
when past invades present
instead of being done

in my mind I called him back
over and over
as if he were a fugitive
and I finally found him
in the empty space a voice fills.

Early Autumn

These pre-fall nights scare me
with their clarity

when reds are honest
not masking rage
gold pretends to be milk
pours itself across sky
warming clouds posing
proudly above ocean

sunset doesn't wither or cry
when it leaves

each day starts over
new clouds
flock of birds breaks through
free of burden

blue-grey pall
shadows earth
to veil what ails us.

Soil to Soul

I began to take an interest in dirt
after pouring scoops of my father
at the base of a tree in Santa Fe

it jarred me
how almost identical
are soil and soul
dirt follows us
when we leave a place

later in my airplane seat
I carried him
across state lines
earth and sky underfoot

I bore him everywhere
delicate root
metatarsal to crown
giving me life
seed to heart

remembering he was once
the stately tree
his body column-like
stretching as a wooden axis
skin like bark
first smooth
then cracking with age

in time my father's heart
will branch through me
holding back darkness
as levee confines a river.

Seed

Had I known
he was too tired to live
    would I have gone –
    would I have said –

the last time these flowers
carried an aroma
I was indifferent

each vase has a story
room changes with its contents

now pungent water
in its static container
warns of death
one bloom keeps watch

seeds of orange and yellow mums
from our overgrown garden
saved in a paper bag
poised to be of use

mums keep rabbits away
he said with resolve
we placed dried shredded remnants
in a large rectangle around the plants
months later vegetables blossomed

when we scattered him
ash and bone
I pretended he would return.

Swan Song

The sound of his voice
haltingly musical
like staccato
barely fills a quarter note measure
my breath is effortless
I inhale, exhale fluidity of a full string section

he whispers the stealth of dying
in andante modality
I want to ask him
what is it like to give up every minute
like it's his last
we egg him on
impudent conductors
smacking the baton

hold! hold!
keep pushing that bass
overpower your light wind solo
your huge metronomic 4:4 time
no longer has that fierce trill
vibrato negated
mind tortures a body of work worn out
beats in a damaged heart
undefined, waiting
repeat: stay! stay!
your movement changes tempo
a slowing adagio we can't resolve.

Deciding to Go

I inhale his words
like breath I couldn't catch

he tries to warn me
I don't want to be here
not home or hospital
nowhere
I'll tell you when I see you

death is a matter of volition

pensive in the days before he leaves us
secretly holding court for hours
until spirit gives him free passage

just one month earlier
last trip to the airport
different from those summers
when he dropped his sad
little girls at the airport
when our visit ended

this time he doesn't wave
I disappear with suitcase
absorbed into revolving doors
eventual skyward exit

he had kissed my hand
like a gentle prince
waking his beloved
but with no promise of future
ticket for one.

THINGS I WANTED TO ASK

Only Now

I remember things I wanted to ask
now that you are gone

what year did you leave
the mansion of your youth
maids, butlers, chauffeur
for the tall grey building
with window boxes
that high rise across from the high school

how did you survive
the loss of your father
locked in his body unable to speak
a lonely Parkinson's death

did you think of him
during Nuremberg bombing
in shrapnel-darkened skies

were you touching his heaven
Icarus on a mission
thinking he might be close

it's a short snorter you told me
roll of dollar bills taped end-to-end
hidden among your metals, pins, awards
testament of your flights
your crew had signed foreign currency
over drinks

who are those nameless relatives
in photos piled in your desk drawer
you knew everyone's name

found in my recipe box filed after Z
4x6 postcard sent from your honeymoon
your comrade's name stood out
below the 1984 postage stamp

once you had all the answers
family now scattered
list of the lost lengthened
no wonder youth is wasted on the young
time lost or misused

too late to listen closely
ear to chest.

When Clothes Don't Make the Man

The last year of his life
I woke at two a.m.
then again at four
to find my father
in pajamas and snacks
bathed in artificial kitchen light

his obvious joy that I was awake
leached weariness from my bones
he thought I couldn't sleep
but my ear was tuned
to the soft shoe shuffle
of his worn brown slippers
keeping time with the metal walker
clicking on Saltillo tile floors
his saggy plaid bedclothes
wore the man
carrying him into light

what he had worn
never seemed significant
only a sweater
when it was sweltering outside

his voice booming
he would ask for things
arm's length away
when I was elsewhere
turn the ceiling fan up a notch

even with fifteen remaining coats
in the closet by his front door
I cannot feel the tenor of him

I can almost put you back together
soft camel-colored jacket
rests on my sofa like it owns the place
striking, next to yellow forsythias
peering through the window

I want to collect vestiges of you
glasses that no longer sit
on your nose but still have vision
like you, motionless
in a quick nap

these things paused
without flesh
and presence

what if I could open the closed
edges of my skin and enfold you

jacket, hat, glasses
sit at my desk

without mannequin
or answers

will the arms of your jacket
teach me how to pray
if I fold them to meet sleeve and wrist?

Loss Gathers in Pools of Blue

Some forty years ago we left my father
in Houston for a small northeastern town
family divorce of sorts
second floor of an old creaking house
with its long-bowed hall
enticed three little girls to race down
slide into a new life
away from southern chiggers
and doodle bugs
my mother found men's work
answered a real estate ad
men only need apply
she outsold male colleagues
ran circles around them as promised
much like the marriage.

Our corner house seemed haunted
in the dark
my sisters and I imagined
what the unseen bone doctor
really did below us
cemetery across the street scared us
our big eyes watched
night diggers gouge deep
neat piles from the earth
we pretended to understand death
after school
the graveyard was mysteriously flat
suggestion of something final

I looked into a dog's eyes once
as I shut the door between us
leaving seemed final to her
like dense summer rain filling a crevice
washing away chalk drawings
on neighborhood cement

the idea of return absurd
yearly after that
leaving Texas felt like a death spiral
over and over
Bell Telephone offered little solace

I recognize this hurt
dog, child, evaporated sidewalk art
a life turns mourning
into deep ultramarine.

Northbound Canvas

The long journey away from our father
was all we understood
Louisiana, Mississippi, Alabama
Georgia, South Carolina
nameless motels

every state
      arid horizon
      brittle brown
      faded, unfriendly
continuous barren terrain
promising nothing
as we drove away from Texas
marked by orange and teal Hojo signs

new double beds each night
familiar square greasy long buns
fizzy chocolate chip ice cream sodas
always Mummy's choice
revival from Dramamine stupor
blended with unending backseat squabbles

for our mother it was different
Whites Only Jim Crow blemish
spilled onto the landscape
Deep South tainting
the frame of her marriage

as children we only saw the shadows
etched on rearview mirror
slowly disappearing
we had somewhere to be

mother finally catches her breath
little girls hold theirs
as our father's image fades
becoming beige before the paint is dry.

Ace of Fire, Six of Water

Pick a card, any card
luck of the draw

78 tarot cards
message is still emptiness

Ace of Fire
sparks emerge

my heart walks through water
to douse the flame of losing you

was this a missed sign?
brace for movement

come to terms with this rebirth
child without father

spirit-orphaned
feel the heat of singularity

Six of Water
mermaid sisters slip between borders

ebb and flow / earth and sea
I think: life and death

how to learn from sudden exodus?
look at the shadow side

shape between light rays and surface
find transformation

from his life
to this life.

I Am Not This

I am trying it on again
soft light-skinned jacket
that continues to be too big
wishing for appearance
even his arm
cannot be conjured.

No matter what this is
gaping hole in the earth
where nothing is fertile
I am not this.

I am this
fledgling leaf on a plant
almost ready for discard
sun shines
without prompting.

I am weeding the garden
hoping something will grow
there will be a time
when things die
and it's ok.

I am hope with breath
light among stars both
subtle and loud.

Airborne

When a plane takes off
nose reaches up
back end tilts deep
down to earth

I am in two places at once
peeling through layers of cotton sky
wispy
shapeless
yielding
then falling below ground
underworld kingdom
asphalt
rigid
immovable

steel body held by rivets
floats through troposphere
weightlessly looking for landing
navigating for light
in the dark

somewhere in between
my heart pounds out of the cage
looking for lost lives
from this metal womb
it's as close as I can get.

Careless

When I was thirteen
my mother unearthed
an Italian beaded necklace
from her collection of exotic jewels

I watched glistening gold and turquoise
rebound flecks of color in her green cat eyes
my grandmother's shock visible
too valuable to give that child
as if I were invisible
or eavesdropping

once I lost a 1920 sepia photo
of Grannie in girlish bathing garb

that's where fear of losing things begins
holding onto inconsequential things
one Barbie shoe
top of a Bic pen
torn ticket stubs

it was always assumed
I wouldn't take care of my things

now I've lost my father
did I leave him some where by mistake
he just evaporated
like rain on steamy macadam

how can it be
that of all that passed
carelessly through my fingers
only the gaudy 18k necklace remains?

Torch Thistle

You were so proud of that flimsy cutting
forget that you stole it from the grounds
of the Houstonian Club
just a twig of a thing

six months later
your back patio looked like throngs
poised for demonstration or parade
roots connected in underground solidarity

volunteers sprung up along the driveway
more than once
you offered me a cutting
eagerly placed in my carryon luggage
bound for the northeast

it poked through, winking at the gate agent
limp when I arrived home
I plunged it in dirt

everyday it suffered
without your je ne sais quoi

I tended it, stark stalk displaced
green expatriate without country

thinking, what if we could keep cuttings
of our wilting ones?

1000 Year Flood

Water and my father
have always been synonymous
the pool a daily fixture

I swim a half-mile everyday
that's why I've lived so long
born with fins

he plowed through liquid
one arm overhead
mouth half-open for breaths

my sisters and I played in the shallow end
while he lingered in chlorine conversation
with strangers we thought he knew

we climbed all over him
the sea monster lurking on the steps
Daddy watch me, watch this

once fluid with sea legs
age impaired his movement
unleashing memories of strength.

From the paralysis of sleep
I awoke gasping
water became ice

in a dream I am visiting friends on a hill
sliding down a steep driveway
the road a sheet of ice

cars skid slowly like parade floats
lone bicycle spins by as if on a carousel
in the distance a car pile-up

no one thinks about animals that remain
their desperate eyes glance down the road
they circle between my legs

a white wolf of a dog
incarnation of snow, stares at me
I put out my hand to reach

her fear of abandonment
fur feathers flow between my fingers
so this is what it's like to grab a cloud

she tilts her head imploring me to explain
ice became flood
like biblical aftermath.

I'll walk curbside
he had said on Westheimer
we switched places on the sidewalk

it was then I knew
this fleeting protector
would not be forever

when Hurricane Harvey came
a pool formed around his house
shield displaced

thank goodness he is not here
to see the Houston he loved
underwater

just like in the movies
he would say
fluttering his eyelashes.

Dumfoundling Bay

It's raining over half of Miami
split over the bay

dichotomy of the spirit
sun and nimbus compete

half-harmonious
thunder and joy in the same breath

bay prepares for greying
line down its center

manatees refuse to surface
seagulls refuse to land

is this what it's going to be
same view from every window?

change engulfs a landscape
stops the heart for a time

we move through grief's currents
spill tears, they recede, always returning

what dominates
disguises itself as cleansing

yet blue sky still
pokes through horizon.

C.O.D.

Boxes flood in with promised family silver
majestic candlesticks bent in transit
pepper shakers once carried by gloved
butlers before the Crash

careful, deliberate handwriting
folded pages of schematic drawings
pre-war, then post-grad

his penmanship hadn't aged
from boyish notes to government pleas
for war-induced disability

spiral notebooks smell of musk
growl like lions as I turn each page
odor of a life dismantled

more boxes birth to death
92 years of collected history
war medals, ribbons, coins

unidentified relatives
staring from inside cardboard
photos of women he loved

some he married, those he helped procreate
and antique faces who disappeared

I make piles in preparation
of discarding him

inside files, alphabet comes alive
breathes life into written notes
indelible testament resisting removal

Roget's Indelible: adjective
cannot be eliminated, forgotten, changed
indelible memories of war
indelible influence of a great teacher

I want to understand him
war pilot, academic, serial husband,
inventor, lecturer, father,

political soothsayer.
I become henchwoman
a judge of rubbish

what stays and what goes
who was he, I ask
help me gather these pieces
return-to-sender, make him whole again.

MEND WHAT'S BROKEN

Toy Closet

> All is but toys; renown, and grace is dead;
> The wine of life is drawn, and the mere
> Lees is left this vault to brag of.
> — Shakespeare, *Macbeth*

The ceiling is the sky
board games stacked above the clouds
anything goes here

unpaired doll shoes, game pieces
shipwrecked accessories
waiting for reunion

dolls march off to church in the sea
Barbie cars become boats
plow through waves to new adventures

row of stuffed animals, some torn but loved
Spareribs the one-eyed dog rescued from
refuse pile watches from high shelf

grown up now she closes her eyes
within chaos lives whimsical order
recalls the clean-up-this-mess command

pictures the last house of her parents
safely inside high-fenced yard
fortress between two little-girl chambers

travels back to the magical closet
sits cross-legged on the floor
to mend what's come apart.

Coffee Milkshake

– for Carla who brought joy in his last hour

She had driven across town
that hot summer day
bought your favorite
offered little icy tastes
frothy and always satisfying
in a bed with tray, window, linoleum
in the yellow room
you sipped and retreated stealthily
how you must have felt
eyes closed between mouthfuls
cold ice cream contrasting with
the warmth of some distant light
behind your eyes.

In the intimacy, she sensed distance
a mysterious taking-in-the-moment
five weeks horizontal
now agitated
your blankets kicked off
immune to needs
you slipped through layers of stratosphere
like bed sheets stacked
every swallow catapulting you
to another course
the flavor of this hour
eluding you

body letting go
out of minutes
last supper
time to go
final sip
all gone.

Before Reading His Letters

Even before my birth
that you would someday cease to be
was unbearable. Now you are words
on paper I have not yet touched.

I relish delving into your chronicles
of bomber pilot training
yet this half-inviting stack
is my final flight to you.

Opening the first folded page
I recall in your final month you asked
when are you coming?
not until October, I said.

Oh shit! as if you meant *that's too late
I'm leaving soon to that dying place*
I felt that once on morphine
my eyes opened and closed

like an old cash register drawer
feeling the pull between two places.
I'm steeling myself to read about you
before artillery, old age, final separation.

Your twenty-year young handwriting
bled through each brittle envelope
parchment postmarked 1943
is there a message I might not want to know?

Will I know you before
you ever imagined me
will reading the last letter feel
like closing the book on your history?

The Letters

After his final descent
I breathed a long weariness
the first and last of him
if I race through
what's next?

War years held with frayed rubber band
youthful soldier inside
skillfully climbing each night
through flak-flecked sky.

Zealously reading
flying blind without my wingman
a few letters at a time
rationing to slow the pace
pretending I have eleven missions
to fly through his life.

Dropping food to the starving people in The Netherlands, 390th crews flew six missions carrying tons of food during "Operation Chow Hound" at the end of the war. The windmill in the lower photo was used as the "target" for a drop.

Pilot and First Lieutenant, Arnold Singer from *Cocaine Bill* 1945

Jacket emblems

390th Bombardment Group

570th Squadron

8th Army Air Force

Service photos 1943
B-17G *Cocaine Bill* in background

Our Men In Service

In Final Offensive

2nd Lieut. Arnold M. Singer 21-year-old B-17 Flying Fortress pilot, above, the son of Mrs. Rae Singer of Larchmont Acres, Larchmont, was in action with the Eighth Air Force during the final phase of its giant offensive against the last remaining Nazi bastions.
Helping to pave the way for Allied Armies into the heart of the Reich, Lt. Singer, formerly a student at Massachusetts Institute of Technology, delivered bombs against the vital German rail centers, oil refineries, factories and military installations. A number of times he braved vicious enemy flak and fighter opposition to carry out bombing assignments.
Lt. Singer serves with the veteran 390th Bombardment Group, which has been cited by the President for skill and daring in battle, and shares in another Presidential award for aiding in the Third Air Division's epic shuttle bombing attack on key Messerschmitt plants. The Group holds a war record for destruction of enemy aircraft by a lone group in a single engagement, having shot down 63 German fighters over Munster, Germany, on Oct. 10, 1943.

WWII Homecoming article 1945

The scattering place 2015
Santa Fe, New Mexico

Do not go gentle into that good night,
Old age should burn and rave at close of day;
Rage, rage against the dying of the light.

– Dylan Thomas

Acknowledgments

Gracious thanks to Le Hinton, editor, for publication of "Soul and Bone" in *Bards Against Hunger: An Anthology of Pennsylvania Poets*.

Gratitude to Walter Dolen, publisher-extraordinaire, for his knowledge, technical savvy and perseverance in believing in this project and bringing it to life.

Many thanks to my moxie poets – Heather Thomas, Sandra Fees, Lisa DeVuono – for polishing and encouraging the birthing of this difficult subject.

Much appreciation to Christine Rolland, Normandy, France for her advice on poetic technique using her vision as a writer, sculptor, painter and curator.

Deepest love to my siblings Lisa, Jacqueline, Reagan and Carla, who inspired me and took care of our father at the end of his life.

Photo credits (by author unless specified)

pages 21, 35, 36, 85, 86, 88, 93 – family photos

pages 84, 87 – photographer unknown

The Author

Susan Singer Kerschner is the author of *The Shoulders of Country Roads: My Journey from Head and Neck Cancer*. Her poems have appeared in several anthologies: *Bards Against Hunger, An Anthology of Pennsylvania Poets*; *The Burden of Light: Poems on Illness and Loss*; *Shirazad*; *Arts Connection*; *Bard Fest Anthology*; *Circle Magazine*; *River Poets (Lily Press)*, and *The River of Bucks County, PA*. She was featured in the Berks Arts Council Poets & Painters exhibit at the Reading Pagoda Gallery and won two awards in Summit Arts Fellowships, Schuylkill County, PA. She was a judge for ten years for the Young Poets Competition K-12, Berks County schools, PA and holds a Bachelor of Arts degree in English/Creative Writing from William Smith College. She lives in Pennsylvania.

www.ingramcontent.com/pod-product-compliance
Lightning Source LLC
Chambersburg PA
CBHW050040080526
44586CB00014B/1390